salmonpoetry

And There Is Many
A Good Thing

~~JON TRIBBLE~~

Published in 2017 by
Salmon Poetry
Cliffs of Moher, County Clare, Ireland
Website: www.salmonpoetry.com
Email: info@salmonpoetry.com

ISBN 978-1-910669-62-4

COVER IMAGE: "The Blue Leaf" by Allison Joseph © 2016
COVER DESIGN & TYPESETTING: *Siobhán Hutson*
Printed in Ireland by Sprint Print

for Allison, always, and for my family

To Heidi,

In admiration for all
the good things you
bring into the world!

In friendship,

Jon

2/9/17

Acknowledgements

Acknowledgment is made to the following publications for poems that originally appeared in them or are forthcoming.

Alaska Quarterly Review — "The Divine"

And Know This Place: Poetry of Indiana — "Center of Gravity," "Indiana Marriage," and "Lucky Life"

Blue Mountain Review — "Temporary Landscape"

Campbell Corner Language Exchange — "The Canals of Mars"

Concelebratory Shoehorn Review — "Guantanamo"

Contemporary American Voices — "The Scarab's Tracks"

Crazyhorse — "Nel Blu Dipinto di Blu," "Of Light and Love," and "Ostrich in Your Future"

Fledgling Rag — "Chalice," "Demonstration," "Then, Now, and Later," and "Underwater Medicine"

Iodine Poetry Journal — "Banner Days in America" and "Bethesda"

Narrow Chimney — "Kuda Bux" and "Room Service"

Ploughshares — "And There Is Many a Good Thing"

A Poetry Congeries from Connotation Press — "Spirit Currency"

The Poetry Mail — "Pearl Street"

Prime Mincer — "Surrogates"

Prime Number — "Midnight Rainbows from Devil's Kitchen"

Riverrun — "Noticias del Mundo"

South Dakota Review — "Long Stories About Short Pigs"

Sweet Jesus: Poems about the Ultimate Icon — "Kung Pao Christ"

The Whale — "Leisure," "Pharaonic Tongues," and "The Voice Outside"

Where We Live: Illinois Poets — "Gifts Inside & Out" and "Unexpected Light"

Whetstone — "Current"

Contents

I.

II.

III.

I.

The Divine

for A. J.

I cannot sing but I can listen—
the voice of notes reaching and stretching,
testing the muscles of what sound can be,

should be if we were only ear, only hearing
clear and transcending the clamor of city streets'
rough malodorous push and shove, the traffic

of life's *be there-should have been-yesterday-*
tomorrow morning,... but if the night
were the warmest cave, the primal blanket

to layer and comfort our tired feet, to feed
a flame of shadow and light together,
then pure, yes, pure tone would be the echo

and resonance, the neverending claim to live
in the lasting growl and coo of her voice
as "My Funny Valentine" fades and never disappears,

as the final note possesses Sarah Vaughan, possesses us,
documents the sound we should define as pain,
as regret, as love and loss, as human.

Of Light and Love

Por toda la hermosura
nunca yo me perderé

Inside, the dust and light pattern
        adobe walls and the tears
of wax once candles are cold

beside a wooden altar. Miles south
        of the cases of dingy beer,
shiny boots, and boys crowding

the streets selling tamales, grass,
        forced smiles, this road runs
out with nowhere but North to turn.

This chapel—the only shade—gives
        way to age and cheap Yankee
electronics works where penitents

turn transistors in their hands, place
        their wafer-thin time cards
on the tongue of the clock. Half

a world away my father descends into
        the Rift Valley, the steady low
of two heifers anchoring the ancient

truck to the road. My mission is just
        to find my way back to Nuevo
Laredo, where nothing is new and old

friends dry out from mescal, cerveza,
        and the heat of border clubs
laced with ecstasy and sweat. There

was little night to drive through
          when I left, and the morning
crossings of goats took me near

fields where hunters dropped hundreds
          of doves an hour, raining
carcasses down on village children

scattered across the fields like they
          are the hunted. They tear
some birds apart in their scuffles,

but there are always more falling.
          My engine, morning sun,
and the road all conspire to stop

my journey south here, where pinyon
          and acacia give way to
a dry creek bed of chalky stones

that seem to sponge my very breath
          from the air. In the rubble
of the chapel doorway I look for

scorpions, but there are only stunted
          crosses drawn in red, graffiti
I can't make out. On the walls

inside, *Jesus, No Mas* in large black
          letters stains one side,
a couple of cold campfires near

the other wall beside rags, cans, and flies.
          I've nothing of my own to add,
my father's stories of rain on tin

roofs in Mexico City all that have
        brought me this far—the steam
he saw snaking up from the shimmer

and the children cupping their hands
        in the streets. I want
to be where he's been, but I won't,

I know, and as I shuffle through these
        broken bottles and scraps
of newspaper, the only words I could add

to these walls would be *En una noche
        oscura con ansias en amores
inflamada*, oh happy luck flight!

Juan de Yepes, son of a weaver, you
        would know this place, would
understand these peoples' absence—

conversos like your family had been
        to a new religion of power.
In the cupboard of your imprisonment

you became bent and scoured by your
        brothers' whips; you gained
the scars your second name might

have foretold. In Málaga a nun claimed
        you kissed her through an iron
grille, but your lips were soon to

be quit of this earth; your songs
        and love and name all
that would be left when the crowds

finished tearing at the rags and
        ulcerous flesh you had left
behind. When your corpse was exhumed,

its sweet limbs scattered across Spain
        and Juan de la Cruz was
legend. But your songs show a man,

a man who would know this empty chapel
        and its litter of faith,
the belief in exile, pain, redemption

that drives us all forward toward
        one another. While I sing
in this skeleton of a church, my father

stands outside a shack where seven
        women read their Bibles
by the light from the doorway.

He'll listen to the music of their
        voices till there is silence
before he calls them forth to receive

the cows he's brought. On the road
        back he'll open a paper
sack one of them gave him *for friends*

we do not know, and he'll find six
        brown hen eggs nestled
together, still warm. When he tells me

this I'll cup my hands and pull it
        all close to me; the distance
we speak across will be stretched

tight between us so the shortest step
        will reach halfway.

Then, Now, and Later

The life you lead is not the one you planned;
the unexpected twists have only grown;
your destination changes as you go.

So let the disappointment you feel show—
no pains or sorrows need be met alone.
The life you lead is not the one you planned.

You'll be surprised when someone's outstretched hand
will reach for you. Others can see and know
the unexpected twists have only grown.

The future's less a promise, more a loan
against the time you find your own command;
your destination changes as you go,

hold on to what you can; let the rest flow
like water slips to nothing in dry sand.
The unexpected twists have only grown;

the life you lead is not the one you planned,
there is no roadmap for this shifting land.
Love, hope, and loss can never be controlled;
your destination changes as you go.

Demonstration

I learned your world order then.
—Les Murray

Outside the ABC Cinema they congregated—
seven at most, three hardcore on all days
rain or wind—their innocuous placards raised

high if reporters showed, though usually
slumping beside the concrete wall as one
or two would chide the latest patron seeking

to enter past their protests. *My God isn't
on that screen and neither is yours*, and
Jesus is not a laughing matter, they said

the first and second times I slipped inside,
but the third and fourth they wrote me off
as lost or an employee, which probably were

the same in their eyes. I don't know what
they would have thought had they known
it was Eric's sister, her red hair's brilliance

chiaroscuroed by the concession's neon
pitches for popcorn and Goobers and Coke,
her laugh easy for a sixteen-year-old boy

to mistake for something eternal, something
more than the boredom which sets in between
matinee and evening shows. Still, I paid

only twice, and though I did not then watch
Monty Python's Life of Brian from its genesis
to revelation, I would venture into the back

of the theater whenever the manager was in
the lobby, and so I saw Graham Chapman's
Brian when he opened his window and stood

exposed before the throng waiting for his
divine word, for some holy answer to unravel
the bewildering predicament of their lives.

Room Service

The glass like a tympani rumbles rain all past forgetting,
past the papered streets and inaugural parties,
echoing half-legible phone messages ciphered beyond
any return. Coffee warm and slow as a listless morning
sweats off its last heat, crisp *Post* knifing headlines
across the blank napkin, the dry sweet bun shadowing
cream and sugar. Captive in the wrap of sheets,

he stirs and settles in the early time before chatter
and accounting take full measure, paste the past's events
all over like playbills for last night's final performance.
Gathering the covers' train about his feet he curls in silence,
counting the rings of next door's wake-up call, guessing
the height and weight of the occupants as bodies rise
from the beds around him, stagger out in resurrection

and dumb inertia to each new day's malingering insistence.
Between his breaths he wonders at sights behind his eyes—
pyramids, rivers, the crepe-like surface of orange peels
as wasps weave and dip in the syrupy air of an orchard,
the careless stretch of black leather as a figure pauses
beneath a flickering streetlight, the glint of water
in puddles scattering under passing midnight traffic.

Guantanamo

The shadowed fists of horizon break
north of the Cuban sunset and Gitmo's

just a plain of wind and doubt holding
back hungry and tired tides of current

fortune, policy in the making folded
tight as military corners, tighter than

the hard knot of your heart releasing
and compressing need and remembrance,

solitary pain of separation as a wife,
a son or daughter growing, swells

behind the jut of clouds forcing on
night, the flat slick sea listless and

void as that dark standard limp above
this armed camp, descending with each

plaintive note into the automatic motion
and sure hands which know no other way.

Underwater Medicine

I can't see you through silver clouds of fish,
dark veils of algae tangle between us until
your faint trail of bubbles disappears and I
surface to find the water glancing back
only my solitary reflection. And if for now

it's just my face on the side of a frosted stein
of black and tan, the bubbles' carbonation
floating up to the head as you pour yourself
another and sit back to tell me how the Navy
will train you to dive with welding crews

on offshore platforms in the North Atlantic,
or station you on submarines running silent
for months so no one can find them, I want
to understand your need for this submersion
in a career I thought would take you

into wards, ERs, and ICUs, places you'd help
others hold together bone and blood and breath,
not hooked up yourself to this iron lung of
diving apparatus. In emergencies they'll fly
you out over open water to jump in full gear

where they think the sub waits to let you
in through torpedo tubes, and, as you assure me
they've only lost one man in forty years,
I can't help remembering a young man on
the D.C. Metro with his Pentagon clearance tag

on the wide lapel of his suit who kept declaring
to the woman sitting beside him doing the *Post*
crossword that he was the only one who knows
where all our subs are at any given moment.
As boys, we made seine nets to drag through

local ponds, revealed worlds of diatoms and
plankton under mirror microscopes, watched films
of underwater volcanoes flaming into steam,
and you even sent off a dollar and a quarter
for a piece of real coral. But now we know

reefs are sharp and treacherous, not like
that novelty you carried as a talisman,
and the only silt we're concerned with settles
at the bottom of these bottles of stout and ale
we're emptying. It's not going to change

how you feel, but each time you say the Navy
needs doctors ready to go under, I want
to hold you back, whisper I can feel tides
sucking in like heavy breaths. You'll learn
the language of oxygen/hydrogen mix,

the threat of nitrogen narcosis, the benign
shadow of the napoleon fish and knife-like
silhouette of barracuda, but I have no answers,
only my hope your tanks will always be full,
that you'll be watchful, patient and surface slow.

Bethesda

No notes, no cards, no correspondence can fill
the space open in this empty house, bed sheets
slip over your belly rising like a domed monument
languishing beside the Potomac, echoes passing

this inactivity of morning like a second heartbeat,
the sleepy circles of your hand's reflex caressing
a spot from the last kick, a fever dream movement
burnishing the dull ache to solitude's shiny pill

of longing, and regret is the cedar's harassing
grackles, oily even in the eight o'clock heat,
quarreling for late summer leavings they mill
about the back yard, soil the street and pavement,

chattering through the silence of resentment
and the brass buttons gleaming from the dressing
table, chevrons arching beside them as if to will
the closet's blank dress white uniform complete.

The Scarab's Tracks

for my niece

In Maadi, sunrise shifts heat
across ragged palms, bending

their rigid poses like divers
arching back in perfect

falling motion. Behind the jigsaw
four-foot stone wall, Katherine

spills cool water over impatient
poppies, cleansing dusty petals

bright as sirens, bright as her
fine hair seared white-gold molten

by morning's arrival. She coaxes
fat red wasps down about her,

untwirling a sweet bun like
an African river wrinkling its way

past crocodiles and staunch
secretary birds, twisting and

lapping into dark alluvial fans
unfolding rich deltas, feathers,

graveyard bones of banyan and
lost ivory. Katherine pinches

back anthills at her sandaled
feet, traces a beetle's tracks

with her big toes furrowing
the sand right up to the shiny

carapace glistening over its
ball of earth. In the kitchen, her

mother soaks tomatoes in a warm
sudsy sink. She'll peel them later

and she and Katherine will turn
the sweet pulp on their tongues,

taste late summer in the flesh
and seeds of the luxuriant fruit.

The Canals of Mars

Cradling their daughter like she balances
on a swing between them, my brother and his wife
calm and cajole the four-year-old as she screams
out her frustration at the Gordian knot dehydration
and peanut butter have tied inside her bowels,
locking off all but the thin stream of disappointing
urine that wind and sand dismiss the way rain
might be rudely met if ever it foolishly visited
the western Libyan Desert. Abandoned land mines
could spot the shards of quartz sandstone and red dust
surrounding this slip of road, misplaced or forgotten
adult toys from one pointless border war or the next,
but Danny, the microbiologist's five-year-old,
runs off the safe asphalt and back, a silly game
of dash-and-danger that keeps his mother busy
between the boy's attempts to peek at my niece's
futile efforts. No caravan of spices or slaves or gold,
we've traveled from Cairo past Alexandria
to Marsa Matrouh and now on toward Siwa
in two 4-wheel-drives loaded with Baraka water,
Coca-Cola, cheese and crackers, apples, Juicy Fruit,
cassettes of Billy Joel and Rolling Stones
and Lucinda Williams, bed netting, and Deet
to visit the site of the Oracle of Amun where Alexander
sought ascension as Pharaoh before his Macedonian troops
but turned back after hearing the priest's whispered words.
Who needs Ozymandias where the unbroken plain
speaks for itself, the arrogance of empire no more
impressive here than the carefully-lined path we saw
some twenty klicks back leading to the road
from a small stone house, the only refuge from sun
and searing heat in the imaginable distance.
Someone thought the hundred-odd heavy rocks
marking this stretch of red earth from that
were important enough to plan and gather, pattern
and place to mark this habitation as human,

to say, *I'm here*, despite it all, the desolation
this stretch of territory denies simply with an ordered
line of stones. No wonder stargazers dreamed canals
for that other Red Planet, festooning Mars
with gondolas of gossamer and stardust to sparkle
against the arctic song of space, the reality
of vacuum canceled by the possibility of fancy,
a mind playing out its options in a universe
of long odds. We've been stopping too often anyway
for my brother's liking, the microbiologist's Bronco
losing air in first his left rear tire and now the spare.
While he makes his third change of the afternoon,
I roll the limp wheel to my brother's Trooper,
past my sister-in-law, who has spread a towel
over the road's surface for my niece to rest upon.
She massages her daughter's swollen belly,
and I think I hear her whisper, *Good girl, good girl.*
The dust sifts down across this plain like a veneer
of permanence, unsettled at a glance, but shifting
and upsetting like the boy's continued efforts to find
explosion, flinging stones toward whatever he imagines
waits under the mysterious and seductive earth.

Midnight Rainbows from Devil's Kitchen

for R. G. J.

The lantern dims and sputters the little light
we need to wait in the dark for the lines
to pull, release, pull, and—taut at last—

set the hook and play the catch around
the other four lines waiting, their purpose
to weigh the night in against our careful

measurements and patience. A constellation
of baitfish scatter like some new universe's
primordial moment, the crappie and shad

bumping the nearest poles slink into green
shadows beyond us, and now the headlight
floating in its foam ring illuminates the flash

and run of this twenty inches of muscle
straining against its life's breath burning
up the blood. We'll net and ice the fish

soon, cut the length and spill out what's in
back to dark shelf of oxygen layered cold
below us in the table of the lake, but now

the splash and dash, the leap of color
our eyes can only hope to prism holds
us here until the limit, and brings us back.

II.

Nel Blu Dipinto di Blu

Mrs. Brown sings to the world above me,
Vo-la-re,Woah-oh. Vo-la-re,Woah-oh-oh-oh.
Bigfoot Stacy's not back home from school,
her adolescent feet not yet stomping out
their parcel of territory amidst the chintzes and photos,
the plastic covers and crystal ashtrays decorating
this edge of Queens. Mrs. Brown is happy today,
A man back in the house, though I am decidedly
temporary, cramped between my sister-in-law's
surgery and her impending move from this dank
basement where every corner holds mildew-
and-moisture collectors that are losing their battle
with the swamplands behind another ill-placed tract
of housing. It's cheaper to live in Rosedale's backwater
—especially below groundwater level—but you
breathe the cost of every dollar saved from clammy air,
and if JFK's usual arrivals and departures don't jar
the little peace left from Stacy's restless percussion,
a Boeing coming in low reminds you that what goes up
blasts in hard and loud, quaking cups from tables,
rattling the concrete slab cold beneath socked feet.

I pack days, spend afternoons negotiating the trek
to Long Island Jewish Hospital, where the nurses
appear to work each corridor only every other day
and the young surgeon departed for a conference
in a sunny clime the morning after my sister-in-law's
five-hour, unexpected nephrectomy. Mrs. Brown
commiserates each morning with me over
too-sweet coffee, remembering stories of generous
boyfriends, a husband or two or three, all struck
with withering ailments or sudden deaths that stole
their youth, *So tragic*, she says, *so disappointing*.
Still, she has her mementos—heavy gold beads
cascading down to a ruby cross, rings with diamonds
clustered thick like a honeycomb of brilliant glare,

bracelets of sapphires or opals or emeralds—
my favorite, she says—such a trove of ostentatious glitter
it must be costume, but I nod and compliment,
not sure, but feeling I must be her first captive
audience in years. She speaks at times of Stacy,
What can one do with a girl like that? Stacy's mother
dead from needles and AIDS, Mrs. Brown took in
her only daughter's child, and their fights seem
generationally-correct, to be expected, though Stacy's
tantrums are more like a four-year-old's than a girl
of thirteen, the kicking and pounding shaking
the tenuous light fixture over my head, the accompanying
breaking glass an awkward and angry young woman-to-be
straining against the fabric of this capricious world.

Mrs. Brown tells me I'm the spitting image
of one of those lost paramours, *such a giving man,
if I could only find his photo*, she says, *I'd show you
your other self*, but she can't and so I must trust
the jewelry box to mirror and testify for her ghosts.
Outside, I see Stacy walking back from the bus stop
with a boy her age. She hits him in the back
with her bookbag, almost tumbling him, and she runs
two houses ahead of him. He picks up his daypack
and, for a moment, seems caught between himself—
a boy wanting to retaliate with his fists, a young man
hoping for a first kiss, if not today then some day soon—
and when Stacy waits for him to catch back up,
he does neither; instead, he takes her bag from her,
carries it beside his own, and Stacy smiles at him,
laughs almost loud enough for me to hear her
from her grandmother's living room sofa,
and Mrs. Brown turns her head, leans back against
me and asks, *What are you looking at out there?*

Long Stories About Short Pigs

for R. S. and Hans Christian Andersen

Each story begins and ends with a pig:
The beautiful story in Florence—
the beggar boy asleep on the back
of the Metal Pig fountain on Porta Rosa,

the sluice of late-day vegetable stands
emptying in the evening breeze,
the stars slick in the fountain pool
when the Metal Pig rises, comes alive

like all good statues in all good stories
should, and runs with the amazed boy
clinging to the brass sheen, the forged
muscles surging as the Pig races

through the city's treasures, vital
in the child's innocence and the beauty
of the Piazza del Granduca, David's statue
and Perseus, Venus de' Medici beckoning,

Bronzino's Christ descending into Hell
to release the joyous pagan children,
the Church of Santo Croce and Galileo's
tomb where his mind rested in the ever-

spinning earth, and the Metal Pig and boy
lingering in the Madonna's cast-off light,
though no enchanted pig would dare
to clop across the cathedral floor.

Then there is the other pig—
a pig stumbling into a metal-mind
world where the Chinook cuts jungle
air with blades of hot wind as another

village on the wrong side of a map
in another war empties to bamboo
and rice burning and the sulfur sun
unforgiving as the soldiers sweat to save

refugees who don't understand the day
has turned them out, don't understand
napalm rain will cleanse the insurgent
treeline, and as the second lieutenant

looks up to see the last Vietnamese family
pressed into the metal belly of the cargo
chopper, he spots the black and white
sow punching at the helicopter's padded

walls with a snout frothing to red,
the weight of the pig lifting with the rest
of them into a present with no good
future, commands lost on the father

who saved the animal to save a family,
but they can't speak to each other and
no one can tell a pig feeling the world
move under and around it for the first

time anything, and screams and squeals
and shouting pitches the equilibrium
of the lieutenant back and forward
until the pig before him is the only

thing in the world he understands,
a black and white question with eyes
like the fists beating out of his chest
and down his arms until one hand pushes

back the pleading man, the other pulls
his sidearm and fixes the pig's terror
in the answer reporting from the muzzle.
A pig is never only a pig. When Odysseus's

sailors scuffled for acorns in the ruddy
dust, they ate away the separation we
insist upon between two legs and four,
between the hand and hoof, between

snout and clever, knowing smile.
And the cannibals who distinguished
the long pig of their preferred table
from the short beast of the mud and fields

knew the cut of the flesh transformed
friend and enemy, warrior and priest
locked in the powers of sympathetic
magic and the transubstantial. Of course,

a fairy tale is only a fairy tale and, of course,
the boy who rode the Metal Pig becomes
an artist and finds a life beyond the streets.
But the father and his family and the lieutenant

are left as statues in a raptured tableau where
the angels and demons lift and drag
the Shithook careening on its endless flight
through the torn sky into heaven's furnace.

Kuda Bux

Hindu mystic, I watched you thread needles
blindfolded, the bandages, tin foil, lead
swathed about your head like a bad dream.
A baker wrapped your face with dough,
yet still you centered the dart to its

bull's-eye, floating the silver plume
across the fuzz and sputter of our Philco's
dusty screen. My sister and I huddled
beneath the glow like that pup waiting
for his master's voice. Instead we heard

Rex Marshall those Saturday nights—before
he went on to *Circuit Rider* and America
for Christ, Inc.—as he introduced the man
with the X-ray eyes and the lovely Janet
drew back the curtain to unveil the miracle

of Kashmir. I agreed with the girl who said
Kuda Bux saw through his nose, my sister
with the little boy who believed Kuda
swiveled his whole head around and peered
out the back. Those years before color,

years before Mary Martin would lift off
the stage, become a boy who never grows old.
"Whatever happened to Norman Fell?" I ask
as my husband settles in front of *Three's
Company* re-runs, watches Chrissy jiggle

his lust young again. He doesn't know—
I doubt anyone knows—but I remember
squinting through the fumes and dust of Indy
and Norman Fell perched on the back of
the pace car. The brickyard echoed the chant,

Staaanleey! Staanleey! You getting any,
Stanley? And I think I joined in; I must have.
He waved and smiled and we all loved him
for making our own failures insignificant.
Now, my sister's children think I'm an '82

Impala wagon, fake wood side paneling
pulling up in their driveway Saturday mornings
so their mother can go to Jazzercise, vinyl
beige interior they can pile into to go
anywhere. I've got ninety-five thousand

four hundred and seventy miles on me,
but I'm still running. I'll turn over
that odometer some day soon, but will it make
any difference? What if it did? What if
we could start fresh every hundred thousand

miles, tune the engine and line up new sponsors
to plug us into their programming block
pitching corn oil and cigarettes to broadcast
fifteen minutes of magic into the ether, roll out
on a bed of nails, or disappear up a rope

snaked out of the air of our imaginations? I'll take
half past the hour or a quarter till, turn back
on the mystery of a wry smile and the silent
nod as my sister's fingers cover my eyes,
my face closing in the mask of her hands.

Pharaonic Tongues

Hieratic script surrounds the statue's base
like armies of black ants attacking the soft

obsidian that has settled on this bare plain
erased of all other features by unrelenting

insistence of wind and sand, conspirators
with time to consume all evidence of life.

And yet these words remain today for us
to touch the rough demands of forgotten

dynasties, workers who braved the sun
to leave nothing of themselves in the terse

sentences praising battles with dubious
outcomes, the exaggerated lives of kings

and queens less revealed by these lines
than by x-rays that strip away wrappings

to reveal encephalitic skulls, perfect teeth,
and the hermaphrodite's misshapen form.

This monument remembers the locusts
darkening the land with a hungry cloud

that stripped the gardens of tender leaves
and blossoms like flames, it sings morning

songs of dawns when the moon and sun
shared the sky as cranes dipped down

to write their passing in ripples dissolving
across the sacrificial lake, it commemorates

the bodies of children piled underground
like a cache of scrolls to be unrolled one

day to document treasures long to dust—
knowledge no longer worth passing down.

Noticias del Mundo

Today her dress flares white,
and in this South Texas heat
I almost lose her in the mirror
of the sweaty street. But

she's coming here, she'll cross,
she always does. I can tell
by the bruises if they've

capped off another rig, if he
sits brooding at home, waits
for her to bring *tripas*, some
potatoes, a job he might work

for a week or two, till
oil's pumping steady again.
And I don't hate him because

he hits her—I can't say I'd
never find myself wiping back
tears I caused—but I still
hate him, the way he could

cross the border, return
with a cousin's daughter, an
in-law's sister, the way she

stands and reads the Mexican
rags I get a week late from
Distrito Federal, the way I
let her read longer than I should,

the way her yellow dress Friday
was caution, neither *stop* nor
go, the way her legs today warm

through the white skirt, cast
shadows of heat across us both,
the way if we stood together
someone would sneer *illegal*,

another *gringo*, the language
that we can't share across
a smile, a nod, some change.

Ostrich in Your Future

Dancing as the smiling animation
to pitch a late-night infomercial
of sure quick money, these feathered livestock

lay a new nation daily from Calgary to Bakersfield,
the Rio Grande to the Wabash Valley;
hatching blue necks paint the dreams

of twenty-first-century cattle barons,
pillowing their sleep with Cognac and Winter White,
Black and Buttercup leather—quill-patterned,

of course, for stylish boots and Western wear,
hatbands and accoutrements for the fashion savvy,
and feathers like God's own fingers,

beautiful, durable and static-free
for dusting the latest microchip technology.
But the true ostricher knows it's meat—red meat—

that feeds America's maw, and these overgrown pullets
drop it in pounds in the slaughterhouse,
steel floor swilling in the bird's life,

the carcass transformed to an alien landscape
of spongy and slick, the tongue of muscle lapping
the dark sheen of stomach and liver,

the trails of intestines never ending.
The brown hens cluck then bow
in awkward submission to the male's thump

and bellow, but it's the camera that truly loves the bird,
from clownish-faced adults to newborn
spraddle-legs, the sensual eye lingers

to pan the length of inviting leg to massive thigh,
to the unfurled chest and lazy river of neck
stretching out of focus, lens marketing personality

beyond grinning beak and absurd wings
that lift no bulk but air. Full and empty eggs
are candled for the shadow of life's gesture

or its absence; dried blown shells are colored
for endtable knick-knacks, varnished half-moon shards
hardening for ashtrays—no waste, no bother—

and a kickline of tongue-wagging birds onscreen
morph into prancing dollar signs, 800 # flashing,
operators standing by for your call.

Banner Days in America

My first flag burning went by the book,
the fabric worn and tattered, the flames
clean and only a proper measure
of respect for this particular spent
emblem that could no longer wave
above us without trailing threads
of glory, a sieve looking shotgun-thin
to a slight breeze. The next time unfurled
dramatically with no real flag at all,
purple mimeographed stars and stripes

with "No Blood for Oil" slashed across the sheets
with permanent red marker, and we
crumpled and tossed them in a trash can
burning our outrage in a small Midwest
college town where the sheriff left well
enough alone as long as we stayed orderly
and there was no real property damage.
I know it's unlikely I'll wage war,
foreign or domestic, in this lifetime,
but don't look to me to wear out

the red, white, and blue on lapel pins
or bumper stickers, on a T-shirt or
blazoned across my backside; I won't
put my hand over my left breast, but
I'll probably stand from training
elementary school left conditioned
in my customs like smiling or wiping
my feet. Such ceremony is suspect
when push shoves me into "love-it-or-
leave-it" hardline rhetoric, and I'll

let someone know that the right fender's
appropriate to parade down Main
with Miss Tyson Chicken perched on
the back of a white Caddie, that a draped
casket like my Uncle Billy's should
place the blue canton over the left
shoulder at its head. I wish I were more
sure that red really means hardiness
and courage, blue stands for perseverance,
vigilance and justice, but I have too many

doubts about the white's purity,
the problems that presents. Still, I know
the military fold and hearing reveille
I can remember racing the sun
into the sky with sure hand-over-hand
motions hoisting the limp material,
and "Taps" will always remind me of
the two folds lengthwise, starting at
the stripe end and triangulating the cloth
till the cocked hat almost clicks into place.

Leisure

One of the cats licks the carpet,
tasting the hidden flavors of days
and nights in the knotty fibers,
while I read out loud a poem
of rapture and sorrow. The cats'
owner wrote this poem and
she sends bright postcards
of the Alps where she and her
husband have only found rain,
cold and damp, diminishing
the Continent. I cannot tell
if this gray and white and tan
cat recognizes any echo of
her owner's voice as she rolls
back and forth exposing her
snowy soft belly. Her sister
rests downstairs, though I'm
not sure if she sleeps—now
or ever—her yellow eyes
seeming always to squint
slightly open. She does
visit me at night as I lie down
and she climbs across my shoulder,
plants herself in the crook
of my left arm, an alert weight
holding each shuddering
breath still, anchoring the body's
drift through sleep and dreams
of ancient blue mountains
tumbling back to earth, filling
the valleys with crushing waves
of stone and ice, a rumbling
avalanche waking me as sirens
pass in the dark street. With her
white paws crossed beside me,
her black back pressed firm
against my chest, she shivers
with this slight turn, but remains.

Current

I.

Bleeding Tooth, White Dwarf
    Turban, Unequal Spoon,
        Turkey Wing, Golden

Olive, Lovable Nut, Fragile
    Scallop, American Bittersweet,
        Paper Mussel, Glassy

Teardrop, Tulip, Polished Scotch
    Bonnet, False Jingle, Gaudy
        Spindle, Dogwinkle, West

Indian Pointed Venus, Fat
    Dove, Cylinder Sundial,
        Alphabet Cone, Flame

Helmet, Partridge, Crosse's Tun,
    Pisa, Coffee Bean Trivia,
        Paper Fig, Flamingo Tongue,

Leaning Dwarf Triton, Angel
    Wing, Carved Star, Stiff Pen,
        Sand Pandora, Spiny

Cat's Paw, Checkerboard, Sunray,
    Blackberry Snail, Blood Ark,
        Shiny Auger, Gem Turret,

Snowflake Marginella, Little
    Green Razor, Jewel Box,
        Noah's Punctured Shell.

II.

I mean jesus! it was lying
there on the beach,
I mean it was washed up,
still in a sneaker.
Probably Brownsville,
everything on Padre floats
up from there. I patrol,
watch for speeders, check out
girls, one of them
screaming, pointing
at this clump of seaweed
but it isn't.
I thought of hardheads,
jellyfish, maybe a little
shark—but a foot?
a foot has to come from
somewhere, somebody!

News trucks and I'm
bagging the thing—
almost wiggled out of the shoe—
the sheriff talks
like he knows about currents,
the way everything ends up
on this island.
Hell, we'll ship it
to the State Crime Lab
up in Austin.
Nobody here knows anything
about it. Tomorrow tourists
will be out on the beach,
looking for other parts,
collecting sea glass
and shells, sand dollars.

But I'll tell you—
after I called it in,
got everyone away and no one
was looking—
I put my shoe beside it
and it was almost the same
size—I swear it!
Somewhere there could be another
foot, legs, arms, a head,
a face floating up
in the backwash of the Gulf.
I kicked dry sand
over my footprint
so there'd be no questions
and waited for the sheriff,
watched the waves turn over

And There Is Many a Good Thing

I went back to Dagger Point Trail
after she moved to Baton Rouge.
A plaque at the point says the sea
takes back five inches a year,
but the sand and shells, the same
live oak still crowned the hills.

I remembered the redtail tearing the rabbit
on the path before us,
wings half-spread, eyes
like sunlight. Linda stooped for a stone,
but a finger to my lips
and a short nod stopped her.
We sat in the dust until the hawk finished.

She drew circles within circles,
leaving only room for a point, like a target.
She laughed when I said she was working against
infinity, and asked me if I thought the rabbit
was the beginning or end of the cycle.
I said, *Neither*, and *Both*.

At the top of the hill
live oak thinned and we saw buzzards
descending on what little the hawk
had left. A collared lizard
stretched on a stone.
It scampered into shade as I stepped toward it.

Tilting the canteen, she splashed water
into her mouth and over her face.
She shook drops from her hair
and arched her head back,
eyes closed, smiling at the sky
like she'd broken surface after diving deep.

Lucky Life

Upriver from Metropolis, its flaking
Superman square-jawed in heavy Illinois
spring, the Ohio's spilled past levees,
dirty water kissing the legs of stilted

trailers leaning back longingly toward
Kentucky from the Indiana shoreline.
The Evansville roads drive right down
to the river, trails disappearing any

season into back-eddying currents
as if submerging is the only answer
to the life these swampy bottoms offers.
Imagine: a boy or girl scrambling up

or out of the aluminum shelters, all
smudgy arms and legs speckled with
the bitemarks of fleas and mosquitoes
breeding in the stagnant backwash:

what Technicolor paints the days and
nights this child passes? A few spindly
antennas crown metal roofs, electric
possibility channeling in *The Price*

Is Right, Wheel of Fortune opulence
shaping these lives to an All-American
mold. Huddled about the pixilated fire,
cartoon promises guarantee *That's all,*

folks! with piggish glee, but is it?
Downstream, Merv Griffin's riverboat
casino rests moored between its nightly
cruises back and forth from debt and

its release, but the short odds belong
to the house. Trotline runners and
would-be farmers gather here with
the semi-pros to rearrange slick chips,

the ruttish numbers spinning orderly
behind the smile of the pit boss.
Captain Fantastic won't be here tonight
or any night, so these luck wranglers

rustle one another, hoping to herd
together a clutch of compliant faces.
Flood or drought, the land sinks here
beneath the economy's tide of desire.

III.

Center of Gravity

The man beside me stares up at television
replays of races that ended three days ago

while paramedics try to hold his son's leg
together. The boy's friends left him pinned

in a car—better not to call the police, he was
drunk, a second DWI worse than death to

them, more real—and the man says he can't
wait to get his hands on them. I skim *Popular*

Science, try to find something in the pages
to convince me of anything more than

the smallness of this place, frustration I don't
want to share with the guy in the DeKalb cap

whose girlfriend's telling the police everything
except, *He hit me. He doesn't mean to, but*

he hits me a lot. When he walks out with her
later, her face shiny with bruises, she stops him

from opening the door, says, *It's too late*
for that, just loud enough for any of us left

here watching Championship Wrestling to hear,
but we're too good at not listening, the only art

any of us has mastered. The nurses won't tell me
how you're doing—*nothing's been determined*—

and they sit around with their coffee and
tell one another how busy they are, how they

can't believe so much is happening here.
No one else in the waiting room and I'm

tempted to turn off the ball game, remember
a friend who said baseball is the perfect game

—no time limit—played perfectly by both sides
a game would go on forever, and I think about

these players giving every last strain to end
things and keep things going. It's a terminal

world, the center only a shifting mass of jello.
Popular Science reported this—researchers

creating computer simulations, astronauts
completing experiments in space observing

globes filled with silicon. They're pleased
how the two appear similar, another proof

in a universe of guessing. They also found
new matter, quasi-crystals that shouldn't exist,

but do, despite expectations, breaking rules
we once thought applied. If they'd just

let you out, we could go home and I wouldn't
think about these things, just hold you against

the pain, bring you water and poppyseed cake
and re-enter an orbit that makes some sense to me.

Pearl Street

You wrap the fish again, so tight the cats
will yowl for days until the garbage truck
lumbers up the alley. South Texas wind

can keep the strongest scents at bay, at least
on days the heat stays down. The window screen
lets in the hint of brine the Gulf gives up

every season here like the taste of rock salt
sometimes would bite your lips when January
in Bloomington got turned to lake effect

Midwestern weather and you were caught out
unprepared for ice and snow and the one—
the only thing—that you could find to scrape

your crusted windshield clear was the black comb
you carried in your back pocket because
your father taught you never venture out

without being prepared to run into
the most important person in your life,
whomever that might be this week or next.

Two friends are waiting for you to join them
in California doubles before lunch,
then drinks at Baby O's, where the afternoon

dancers expect less from businessmen who
wouldn't be here if they had an angle
on anything the least bit promising.

Maybe the cats have it right—if you complain
enough, loud enough, long enough about
that scent that draws you in, the hope you can't

deny even if what they want is only
your trash, what you want is the morning breeze
you know is blowing in right now out at

Bob Hall pier, the clean air whipping the dune
grass, caressing the shoulders of the girl
you know is there each day by eight o'clock,

her yellow towel spread, her ice chest still
full of Dos Equis, suntan oil and sweat,
coconut a liquer intoxicating

anyone downwind, the thin line of beige
across her back where she's unloosed her top,
the flash of light above her thigh's new dark.

Chalice

Every morning's benediction—
          kiss, caress upon shoulder,

     whisper of waking and
welcome to the day. We file

       away the armored faces,
brush off our iron burdens

     in the goblet of this
communion—our bodies, our blood,

       our host of affections and
tears, the lonely fountains

     of our redeeming hours
where we store up enough embraces

in the strength of arms, tender
          smiles beneath tired masks.

Sensual rapture, sufficiently
      holy to *take, eat*—this our

sacrifice and celebration—
         take, drink—this our bond

     and resurrection in life,
love, honor and affirmation of being.

Indiana Marriage

The state did not require my blood
and yours had passed all inquiry
this county seat demanded, so we
hurried back to find the cashier
before she locked up for the day.

It wasn't bad once we figured out
the maze of offices, and, as she
checked our forms for accuracy and
completeness, you noticed half
the fee went to a fund for battered

and abused spouses. The judges
were all booked for end of the year
ceremonies, the mayor and vice-
mayor out of town for the holidays,
so we settled on the city clerk

and waited for the weeks to pass
until my parents and your sister
could get away to witness our vows.
A gray day like most that December,
you wore a purple dress and I

slipped on a sweater, and we drove
the few blocks to the city office
building that looked more like
an old elementary school, orange-
brick facing the only festive touch

of the afternoon. The assistant
city clerk showed up in her tennis
shoes—the clerk a victim of that
winter's flu—but she brought along
a robe for an official touch, and

she led us back to where they kept
the vows, xeroxed sheets where names
were scratched or whited out and
replaced time and again as each new
couple registered their vows and

joined the temporary lexicon. We
chose innocuous words, quick and
direct and without vestiges of
overt possession or obedience.
There was hardly time for my

mother to tear up before we both
said "I do," and we were done.
Two friends who hoped to witness
the event were five minutes late
and we met them and hugged,

and then the wedding party—
such as it was—drove to the town's
only seafood restaurant where
my father treated us all to shrimp
and crab and so-called catch of the day.

As we toasted with our water
glasses raised high, the waitress
brought out a thick slice of Key
lime pie, and we fed one another
a bite of its tart sweetness.

Surrogates

My sister asks my wife to bear her child;
or, rather, she asks me to ask for her.

And that—more than the phone calls she hasn't
returned in six months; more than my knowing

she, her husband, and her son will listen
to my voice wandering through the awkward

messages as I'm leaving them, my words
stumbling into electronic lockup

like a teetotaler blasted on Long
Island iced tea, lurching to an ugly

and confused mess; more even than her new
first name she decided her family—

especially our mother and father—
now must all use when writing or speaking

to her because she knew she never was
really just a "Beth" or a "Beth Ann" but

rather "Elisabeth" spelled with an "s"
so the whistling sound can hiss from teeth and

lips like a radiator warning of
the predicaments of pressure—that choice

she has made to make me this messenger
tells me we have entered our adult lives

either not listening to one another
or not caring. I do not know how I

would feel if I thought my wife might ever
seriously entertain this notion,

how we would pass the nine months (if it took)—
my sister's egg, her second husband's seed,

their idea, their dream incubating as
we, a childless couple with no plans of

changing that situation, waited out
the weeks like a lease was winding down, games

of Scrabble and Boggle between doctor
visits, and then, when the day arrived, how

my wife would feel to lose this tenant, this
piece of not-her separating, turning

to its genetic nest now that the womb
no longer fed and warmed its days and nights?

But this is all academic: when I
lead up to the question whose answer I

already know, my wife's "Hell no" may not
be eloquent, but it is simple, it

is passionate, it is accurate, and
like a letter unanswered, a card or

gift unremarked, there is little room for
misinterpretation, no room for doubt.

Unexpected Light

We drive past signs for Al's Reefer Service
and Throwed Rolls and you want to know
how far we've come since our last stop,
where the next town will slip past into
the almost-imaginary gloom which seems
to crawl its way along this Mississippi Valley
bottomland like those sow bugs at our last
apartment meticulously gathered together
to die in a huddled dusty mass underneath
the maple desk too heavy to even think
of moving. But we have. Moving up
the country's belly and breadbasket,
southeast Missouri-northwest Kentucky
twang droning "heartland" at us,
a mantra of the self-invented middle
thumping its way behind our temples
like ridges on highway shoulders grate
against sleepy rubber for semis veering
out into soybean fields halfway between
Sikeston and Cairo. Wake up into
this dream we've come upon like
the night on this interstate we drove out
into the cold dark to discover the road
in flames, a blazing pickup abandoned
in the far lane, a beacon we spotted miles
before it seared the night with fierce heat
that burned us even through the glass.
Now we see through the unexpected light,
afterimage asking us to accept what we
can't anticipate, not ready to believe
in this mist breaking over burial mounds,
largest cross in North America rising
from Shawnee hills. A map won't tell where
we're going, though you offer the atlas,
tattered and stained from the last trip
or the one before. The odometer will keep

tallying the miles behind, while you
measure the road ahead by exits and
exchanges, highlighting where we need
to get on and off, rest and start again
toward our next definition of home.

Kung Pao Christ

Driven across miles of deer-path highway
to this link our taste buds remember as city
and sizzle, Szechuan and Hunan, even Thai
and Indian buffets on alternating weekends,

we settle in a corner across from the elderly
couple who ask if the Chinese New Year
brings a new calendar, new months, a fresh
marking of the passage of time, and the man's

shaky fedora tips like he's seen enough days
to stop counting forward in any hurry. This
over-extended menu seems just right on a late
January night when smalltown cute, "Kountry

Cookin'" glacially surrounds us like a slow-
moving tomb of arteriosclerosis. But it's only
the graying winter slush—we hope that's all—
until a woman and a boy come in and sit across

from us. He's her grandson we find out over
our hot and sour soup, their conversation bridging
the quiet space between us in this otherwise
empty restaurant all too easily, and they act

like any other generationally-challenged pair
might until after they've ordered the crispy
duck and "King Pa" chicken, and as we split
the order of spring rolls, basting the shells

with mustard and fluorescent orange sweet-
and-sour sauce, they begin their discussion of
the Rapture, or at least what sounds like Last
Days, though the peculiar twists and tracks

of these new Revelations show an inspiration
fitting the end of the Millennium in a cathode-
ray confessional. The souls rising won't need
bodies from the grave but they'll get them

anyway, their flesh like Salvation Army toss-
outs clinging like a net or overcoat to cover
something garbled between the boy's admiring
responses of "Cool" to Grandma's calling

ministrations. He says, "They don't tell us
nothing like this in Sunday school—just boring
Adam and Eve junk." If the woman hears him
it doesn't slow her down while she sinks into

the Bottomless Pit where in her tomorrow we
will perish if we stand with the goats and not
the lambs, where the Beast that is Satan rules
marked and ready to sacrifice pigs against

the tenets of Hebrew Law before he turns to
human sacrifice, one hundred and forty-four
thousand Jewish virgins.... We both hear her
more clearly than the flavors of the cloying

impression of Moo Goo Gai Pan can satisfy
or the black bean sauce lost in bell peppers
and red onions like a Southwestern mélange
of all the wrong tastes in all the wrong places.

As if a perverse angel programmed the five-
years-behind-the-times Adult Contemporary
station subbing for Muzak, a song slips through
the prophetic Babel around us: "Jesus He Knows Me,"

a Genesis hit—a band that sold out artistically
after its lead singer who once was a flower on stage
in those heady art-rock-psychedelic-silly days
left to become Peter Gabriel. No, this Genesis

owes all its glory to the commercial smirk and
swagger, the balding bravado of Phil Collins.
And if music can deliver us from the ways of evil,
from the impulse within to answer the darkness

that is not our own, not our business or belief,
this sarcastic song saves us, gives us strength
to turn our thoughts away from the obvious,
begging intrusion that devils and damns us all.

So even when the crispy duck arrives golden
and spread forth like a cruciform icon the boy
heartily tears from its tender bed of wilting lettuce,
when the patient waiter tells the woman once again

she made the best choice, the spicy peanuts
and meat the restaurant's most requested dish,
cautions her—watch out for the hot red peppers,
please—even when her grandson blurts out,

"So was like Mary a virgin?... That's awesome!,"
and she begins to explain how Mary was "conceived
by the Holy Spirit," we can look away, to each other,
to the cookies like delicate parcels, and fortunes

that read, *You will make much out of a small thing*,
and *You do well adapting in a new environment*,
to the bill and the New Year's token wrapped in red
and gold paper, an unexpected gift, the latest discount.

The Voice Outside

In the courtyard of these dingy apartments
with their fake Vieux Carré facades, a man
beats his love out of a gray locked door,

no tender intimations or supplication
in these poundings that sound all too practiced
in their rhythms—three bursts, a name barked

out like a command, silence, two bursts, silence.
He doesn't care about time, about other
angry or sad or tired or lonely shadows

beginning to rise behind the white and beige
shades, ghost lights flickering, stumbling
to their blank windows to peer out into this

night that is now and forever entirely his,
palpable as the sharp edge of his teeth, his fist
possessing each hurt and budge the wood

won't give. Inside, I hold my wife like sleep
could be shielded by one body ready to throw itself
down on a landmine, offering up breath and bone

to keep the blast at bay. She turns into me
and I try to calm my pulse, the shudder
touching me each time he renews his assault

on the thin walls which separate us all.

Temporary Landscape

I. Monroe County Fire Tower, Indiana

for A. J.

Not easy to see the world
      around us from this tower, even
            though the night stayed clear, the moon

resting full and heavy in the sky.
      But I'm not looking all that hard,
            instead holding on to you ascending

beside me, both of us ignoring signs
      that say, *Keep Off, Climb at Your Own*
            Risk. Here in the middle of America,

the trees insist on turning colors, just
      as locals expect them to do every fall.
            It doesn't seem to matter to any of these

cycles that summer parched us with
      the worst recorded drought in fifty
            years. Perhaps our eyes perceive only

illusion—we'll pay later for this
      false sense of security—but who wants
            to see the future when the present's

so appealing, and I'd like to stay here
      longer than common sense and the cold
            wind will allow. I've told you about

my friends—my real and claimed family—
      scattered across the country, and neither
            of us has an answer to that. Perhaps

this tower stands at a point
      in the center of a web or wheel,
           and these spokes grow out of it,

lifelines connecting me to all
      the places I've touched, all the people
           who have touched me. But now

none of that seems as certain and
      real as the hand warm in my own.
           Climbing down, I test each step

again, and though it's not earth
      I long to touch, the ground still
           feels good and solid beneath my feet.

I'll remain here, with someone
      to hold to amidst the motion of
           a planet quickly spinning, centrifugal

and centripetal forces pushing every-
      thing apart, holding it all together.
           A radio tower keeps pulsing its red

messages to a sleeping world,
      and the stars keep shining clear,
           bright despite all threats of frost.

II.   Padre Island

for D. W.

Lightning arcs and bolts from one rig
to another out on the Gulf tonight,
and this Matamoros wind driving surf
north in an unforgiving tumble squelches
the matches you pitch at our driftwood pile.
We poured enough gas to burn sand,
but you've got to put a light to it
or it will evaporate like these words
neither of us have managed to say. If I

stayed till October I could see fiddlers
march out of the dunes, scribble the beach
with thousands of scampering shadows.
Or I could join you when the flounder
run—you've already got the boat, the rigs
we'd need for the salt flats—you're sure
you could teach me to pop the line
when the fish sucks up on the shallow
bottom and you have to break its hold.

I talked you into a sudden roadtrip to
the Aransas Refuge last March—before
the whoopers migrated back north—and
we sighted one of the last pairs feeding
on blue crabs in the flats. We stood
still and silent as they rose on their
great white wings that I wanted to say
later *shined nothing like sunlight*, but
there was never a need to say anything.

I'll miss that, and more. You finally
get the gas to catch and, for a moment,
flames whip around our bodies and my
breath tastes the burning air separating
us—heat too solid to reach through,
bright inferno I'm unable to see beyond.
While I finish the last Pacifica from the two-
dollar case we brought across the border,
you fling burning wood into the incoming

tide. The fire dead, we head down
toward Malachi, and you start reflecting
on erosion, the way this island reinvents
itself, the way you sometimes can
drive your truck from Corpus Christi
all the way to Brownsville if the sand
piles just so in all the right places.
It's not cold, but I stand here shivering
as the sand keeps on shifting under us.

III.   Pennsylvania Turnpike
    for D. T.

You've never seen a woodchuck before
        so when one rears up
on its hind legs, the fur golden
        in the too-green grass,

you want to stop, turn back, something
        to make sure it's real.
But it's been ten hours on the road
        already, another six

or seven before we reach D.C. You
        haven't left your second
wife yet, and I don't think either of us
        is sure you will, but when

the Alleghenies rise before us and light
        disappears with any radio
station we'd have the slightest chance
        to sing along with, you

start to tell me how you see your
        life—a series of jobs—
salesman, theater manager, bank clerk,
        programmer—all new

experiences to teach you something
        the one before didn't.
And I try to talk about life as
        mission—my father's

years at Des Moines and Nashville
        community centers, my
brother's medicine—but I have no
        room to speak and soon

the only sounds left to us are
        the engine's and silence.
I start fiddling with the radio dial,
        you light up a cigarette,

and when the scratchy refrain to "Alice's
        Restaurant" comes in, we
laugh at each other, neither dumb enough
        to sing along. Stopping

at the first gas station we find in
        Maryland, we wash our faces
in the iron-tasting water from the tap,
        read the lonely messages

truckers left each other in this middle-
        of-nowhere bathroom, and
I know we'll find something better to talk
        about the rest of the way.

IV.   Ocracoke Ferry, Hatteras

for my brother

No dolphins, schools of blues, nothing
in the water except gulls combing the foam
the ferry's screws turn out. When I left
this morning from Portsmouth you'd already
gone, two hours into another day that'd turn
into night and call in the emergency room.

Yesterday it was a surfer you told me about.
He came in with herpes and when he found out
he knew exactly who it was and when. You
asked him if he was so sure *now*, why didn't
he wonder *then*? He shrugged, *You ride
the waves you're given*, like there was no choice

in his life, or yours. I watch the surf here
break into white wreckage on the sand bars
and shoals that make this cape so treacherous.
Back at Kitty Hawk Monument this morning,
looking out over the condominiums and fast food
joints holding this earth down more than any

vegetation ever could, I knew you should be here
with me. But your choice of blood, sinew, and
bone, my choice of books and words define us,
obstacles as real as this violent, ripping wind men
flew against. At Captain Bilbo's, today's catch
is bluefish—very good if you don't eat the skin—

the waitress tells me. And it is good, the best
fish I've ever tasted, meat tender and separating
in white flakes under my knife. I grab a placemat
with the Captain's smiling face, buy a postcard
with *The Gulf Stream* reproduced in miniature, but
I won't give you either. Cars idle in a slow line

when I return to the ferry and I have to wait
for two loads to depart before there's room for me.
The black-and-white lighthouse juts above the blue
channel, and I remember how frightened I felt driving
among the sand hills the first time I hit a break
in the storm barrier, saw the immense water before me,

was drawn toward the sudden flash of white surf
and aqua everywhere catching my eyes, hands,
veering the car toward the pure blue and almost
driving in, off this continent into the deep. On this
boat now, it's less tempting. The rail's solid iron
convinces me enough to lead me back to land.

V. Returning Home

for A. J.

Each breath I take at night seeks to deny
      my life, three hundred and eighty-five
times my lungs closed, stopped, and I woke
      gasping to continue. *Apnea*, they tell me

and so I accept the continuous positive
      airway pressure of 13 cm. to keep my sleep
constant, find delta for the first time
      in ten years, let R.E.M. build a new world

in my head rather than threaten to pull
      it all down. I anchor to this machine,
its hose my claim on oxygen, my elephantine
      surrogate lung pushing air past all my

obstructions. More than any place it keeps
      me alive, yet it keeps me from you.
We tangle together at night, air rushing off
      my face, my mask between your lips

and mine. Could we but kiss away all this
      technology, this physiological wall
inside my throat, I would tie myself to you
      each night rather than it, take the moist

air around us and breathe our lives deeply.

Gifts Inside & Out

The Pinckneyville Business Park
begins with the Correctional Center,
and business is good. For a grand

opening, the warden invited
the townspeople in to test the spring
in the bunk beds, play at prisoner

while a C.O. slid the door shut,
let the sound of freedom's silence
become a ghost note broken by

the percussion of metal on metal.
But no one that night was cataloguing
days, spending as little time

as possible testing the imagined
weight of razor wire, the height
of triple fences and towers

measured in the yardstick of long eyes.
The census takers have come and
gone inside these walls, finished

counting the bodies like cordwood,
tax dollars stored up like fuel
for winter burning. But it is spring

again—redbud and dogwood
flashing along the roads—
and a blacksnake on the asphalt ahead

slides left while my car skitters
shoulder-right, both of us avoiding
a moment of evolutionary end.

The high school's Panthers have been
State Champs before and might be
again; but just past the tracks

on the northside of town, Wickwire
Pre-Cast is going out of business,
their sign no longer promising

*Gifts Inside & Out, only 50% off
or more.* Everything must go,
and most of the ceramic planters

already have, the Virgin Marys
and bears and pigs popular enough
to find a spot in a yard somewhere—

but they made too many deer,
and a herd sidles nervously away
from the road as four muscular

lions stalk closer (their leader
painted gold), a diminished pride
awaiting the sledgehammering

back to dust if another sale fails
to show. Still, there's time
left for a reprieve. Off the square,

the physical and occupational therapist
has added *Work Hardening*
to her list of services, and,

down the street, Kitten's Cafe offers
pie and coffee twenty-four hours a day
every day of the year. But only

a few know for certain what goes on
at the Pinckneyville Coon Club
south of town, the pines and oak

and ragged maples sheltering
the twisting drive back into the hollows
left in the coal-scarred land.

Spirit Currency

for Lynda and Jorge, 1994

Manhattan's jeweled island far back
    below us, the Towers' light like two levers
        you could bend to turn the Earth over,

this jet flies on into morning,
    London somewhere beyond this flat sky
        and jagged water where the toys

that are ships glint out of the moonlight
    and the whale shapes of low clouds
        rise and pass like a call unanswered.

I am leaving behind lives I don't know
    how to speak to in their ending;
        the abruptness of tragedy making present, past

—there is no passing in loss so sudden.
    A week from now in Cairo, I will stand alone
        in a side room with The Book of the Dead

paneled before me while the line
    for Tutankhamen's treasures winds its way
        out of the Antiquities Museum.

No glamour in the embalming rituals,
    Anubis, and the feather weighed against the heart:
        and there are no answers either. Some say fire,

some ice…but the possibilities of death
    are all final, and her accident on slick roads,
        his death in a trailer flaring out in the night

are more now of ending than I can bear.
       She told me editing would teach what I
              didn't need to write, though her own poems

are the lesson I needed most; he barely spoke at all,
       a shy man who let his classmates call him "George,"
              let me call him "Jorge," so when one of them said,

"Did you hear about George?," I didn't know
       who she could be talking about.
              He saved his mother and girlfriend and child

from the water heater's explosion, but, confused
       and uncertain, he went back, found himself trapped
              and screaming, "Get me out! Get me out!"

All anyone could do was help pay for the funeral,
       provide for the needs of the living,
              and none of it could be enough. The legacy

of the lives he saved, the lives she changed
       is the tally we can keep, but we can't measure
              what anyone might continue to become.

Shadowlands begins on the plane's screens
       to wake us into the new day, and as Anthony Hopkins
              brings C.S. Lewis's joy and pain to life again,

I quietly weep with him, holding my breath
       not to wake my seatmate. Wherever we travel,
              there is no destination loss has not visited before us.

JON TRIBBLE's poems have appeared in print journals and anthologies, including *Ploughshares*, *Poetry*, *Crazyhorse*, *Quarterly West*, and *The Jazz Poetry Anthology*, and online at *The Account*, *Prime Number*, and *storySouth*. His first collection of poems, *Natural State*, was published by Glass Lyre Press in 2016. He teaches at Southern Illinois University Carbondale, where he is the managing editor of *Crab Orchard Review* and the series editor of the Crab Orchard Series in Poetry published by SIU Press.